A Funny Thing Happened to Me on My Way Through the Bible

A Funny Thing Happened to Me on My Way Through the Bible

A Collection of Humorous
Sketches and Monologues
Based on Familiar Bible Stories

A Lillenas Drama Resource

By Martha Bolton

Lillenas Publishing Co.
Kansas City, MO 64141

Dedication

To Mom and Dad,
　　For the love,
　　　　the laughs,
　　　　　　and the faith in God
　　　　　　you've shared with me

Contents

Preface

A Funny Thing Happened to Me on My Way Through the Bible is a collection of humorous sketches and monologues based on biblical stories.

It has been said the best way to make a point is through humor, so each of the following scripts seeks to bring forth a spiritual truth by using laughter along the way.

Like the prayer of St. Francis of Assisi, laughter can help us accept those things we cannot change and motivate us to change those things we cannot accept. It is a powerful tool. It can make people stop and think when otherwise they wouldn't even stop.

These sketches and monologues can be performed in a variety of situations such as illustrated sermons, special church services, youth nights, banquets, children's ministries, teaching seminars, Sunday School programs, or, if you're shy, just in front of your own mirror.

The cast requirements are small, and most of the props can be pantomimed. Bible-era costumes are recommended for effect, and a blackout at the conclusion of each sketch seems to work best.

An important point to remember for any stage performance, but especially in comedy, is voice projection. Your audience won't laugh if they don't hear the line. (Sometimes they won't laugh even if they DO hear it, but if that should happen, simply continue with the sketch, and duck a lot!)

Also, don't be afraid to move around on stage. An actor who remains in one spot too long only makes for a good target. Bring energy to the role. As a rule, an audience resents an actor who gets more sleep during the performance than they do.

But, above all else, bear in mind the message in each sketch and monologue. There's something to be learned from "Noah and the Nosy

Neighbor" about obedience. We can see how Jonah's disobedience got him into "A Whale of a Predicament." And in "The Original Superhero," the good Samaritan shows us all how to treat our neighbor. The laughter is fun, but remember it's only a means of getting the audience to consider these truths and, hopefully, begin applying them to their lives.

—MARTHA BOLTON

"Till he fill thy mouth with laughing,
and thy lips with rejoicing."
Job 8:21

Acknowledgments

I WOULD LIKE TO THANK:

My husband, Russ, who honestly believed once this book was finished, I'd get rid of the clutter on my desk.

My sons, Rusty, Matt, and Tony, who have grown up thinking of the typewriter as dinner music . . . and never complained.

Paul Miller, who encouraged me to write this book.

My family and friends (they know who they are), who have always been there when I needed them . . . or at least left their answering machines on.

And finally, all the churches who have let me practice my writing on them over the years. God's people are great laughers!

A Funny Thing Happened to Me on My Way Through the Bible

The Road to Heaven's a One-Way Street

The Story of the Tower of Babel

· A comedy sketch ·

Characters:

BUILDING CONTRACTOR
VISITOR
EXTRAS (*Optional*)

▼

(*Opens with* BUILDING CONTRACTOR *instructing workers. Workers may be imaginary or extras may be utilized.*)

VISITOR (*approaches* CONTRACTOR): Whatcha building?

CONTRACTOR: Oh, just a tower.

VISITOR: A tower, huh? (*Looks it over from top to bottom, then from bottom to top again.*) Can't you build sand castles like everyone else?

CONTRACTOR: Can't build a sand castle to heaven!

VISITOR: You're building this thing to heaven?

CONTRACTOR: Yep.

VISITOR: That's crazy.

CONTRACTOR: No, it's not.

VISITOR: You'll never do it.

CONTRACTOR: Have you tried it?

VISITOR: No.

CONTRACTOR: Then how do you know it can't be done? *(Shouts to one of the workers)* Hey, you! Go back and get a full load of bricks! *(To VISITOR)* You've really got to watch these guys! They're always trying to get by without a full load.

VISITOR: I think you're trying to get by without a full load yourself! *(Taps finger on forehead indicating he's nuts.)*

CONTRACTOR: You're laughing now, but we're going to have the last laugh. We're going to keep laying these bricks one on top of the other until one of these days they're going to lead us to those pearly white gates!

VISITOR: I'm afraid the only white you're going to see is a straight jacket!

CONTRACTOR: You think I'm crazy, don't you?

VISITOR: I think you've been out in the sun too long! *(Laughs)* A tower to heaven! Why, that's preposterous!

CONTRACTOR: I'll bring you a souvenir.

VISITOR: Do you think for one moment that God is happy with your little project?

CONTRACTOR: I don't know. I'll ask Him when I get there!

VISITOR: See what I mean? You're nuts. You can't just climb your way to heaven.

CONTRACTOR: Watch me!

VISITOR: Do you *really* think all you've got to do is build a tower high enough and that'll get you into heaven?

CONTRACTOR: Sure! And if it doesn't work out, we can always open up a nice restaurant with a view. Either way, we're talking about a nice retirement.

VISITOR: But the road to heaven is a one-way street. And believe me, you're going the wrong way!

CONTRACTOR: All I know is we're going UP! So, if you don't mind . . .

VISITOR: I'm telling you, there's only ONE way to heaven, and this isn't it!

CONTRACTOR: Well, we'll see about that! Right now, we're trying to work here. So, would you mind moving your soapbox over just a little?

VISITOR: You're still going through with this, huh?

CONTRACTOR: All the way to heaven. Now, would you beat it? You're starting to get on my nerves!

VISITOR: God isn't going to like this!

CONTRACTOR: Well, that's just too bad, because we're building a tower to heaven, and there's not a thing He can do about it!

VISITOR: Oh, yeah?

CONTRACTOR: Yeah! *(To someone offstage)* C'mon! Hurry up with those bricks!

VOICE OFFSTAGE *(slowly and emphatically):* No comprendo, mi amigo!

The Most Expensive Meal in History

The Story of Jacob and Esau

• A comedy sketch •

Characters:

> JACOB
> ESAU

▼

(Scene opens with JACOB *stirring two pots over a mock campfire.* ESAU *approaches.)*

ESAU: What's in the pot?

JACOB: Which one?

ESAU *(points to pot closest to him):* That one.

JACOB: Laundry.

ESAU: What about that one over there? *(Points to the other pot.)*

JACOB: Stew.

ESAU: Stew, huh?

JACOB: That's what I said.

ESAU: Any dumplings?

JACOB *(giving* ESAU *a weird look):* Dumplings? I think you've been out in the wilderness too long.

ESAU: I'm just hungry.

JACOB: You're welcome to try some . . . (ESAU *starts to get a bowl, but* JACOB *stops him and smiles)* . . . for a price!

ESAU: You mean I have to pay for it?

JACOB: I don't take credit.

ESAU: But I'm your brother!

JACOB: No one said you had to leave a tip.

ESAU (*disgusted*): Well, which one did you say was the stew?

JACOB (*pointing*): That one over there.

ESAU (*goes over and smells the stew; then smells the laundry*): How can you tell the difference?

JACOB: The stew has carrots.

ESAU: You know, you may be a great shepherd, and even an above-average farmer. But you're no cook!

JACOB: Hey, man, if you don't like it, wait till you get home to eat.

ESAU: I would, but I'm famished!

JACOB: So, how much is a bowl worth to you?

ESAU (*takes another whiff of the first pot, then the second pot*): Are you *sure* this one isn't the laundry?

JACOB (*growing impatient*): Do you want a bowl or not?

ESAU: I don't suppose you know what Mom's cooking for dinner—

JACOB: Leftovers.

ESAU: Leftovers of what?

JACOB: Leftovers of last night's leftovers.

ESAU: Oh, it doesn't matter. I'll never be able to wait anyway! (*Goes over to first pot and stirs it*) I'm so hungry I could eat a—(*looks in pot*) Hey, didn't you skin this thing before you cooked it?

JACOB (*looks into pot*): That's my hat! I said the stew pot's over there! (*Points.*)

ESAU (*goes to second pot, looks in, and stirs*): I think I'd rather eat the hat!

JACOB: Suit yourself.

ESAU: Well, anyway, you haven't told me what this stew's going to cost me.

JACOB: I'm willing to make a deal.

ESAU: Yeah? *(suspicious)* What kind of deal?

JACOB: What would you say if I told you that you wouldn't have to pay me any money?

ESAU: I'd say you're up to something.

JACOB: Just give me your birthright and we'll call it even.

ESAU: My birthright for a bowl of stew? Do I look stupid?

JACOB: One thing at a time, Esau! Now, do you want the stew or not?

ESAU: That's a pretty high price.

JACOB: You've always wanted to be the baby of the family. Now's your chance.

ESAU: You just want to switch places, huh?

JACOB: I want your birthright.

ESAU *(looks at stew pot)*: I am awful hungry.

JACOB: Do we have a deal then?

ESAU *(takes big whiff of stew, sighs, then shakes JACOB'S hand)*: We have a deal, little brother!

JACOB: Correction. Big brother.

ESAU: Well, then, big brother, hand me a bowl and stand back! I'm starving! (JACOB *dips some stew into a bowl and hands it to him.*) I sure hope this tastes better than it looks! *(Takes a bite, then spits it out)* There's rocks in here!

JACOB: A few lumps in the gravy.

ESAU: I know! I just chipped my tooth on one!

JACOB: Sorry, no refunds.

ESAU: But this stuff tastes like mortar!

JACOB: A deal's a deal, little brother.

ESAU: But I made a deal for a bowl of stew. This is cement with carrots!

JACOB: A hearty stew is *supposed* to stick to your ribs!

ESAU: Stick to them, yeah! Not break them on the way down! Hey, why's my birthright so important to you?

JACOB: It just is.

ESAU: Well, I get the feeling I just traded away something very valuable for a lousy bowl of stew!

JACOB: You didn't consider it valuable until you lost it. And now it's gone, little brother.

ESAU: But you caught me at a weak moment!

JACOB: I had to. Do you think you'd ever trade your birthright for a bowl of my cooking if you weren't starving??

ESAU: But it wasn't a fair deal. My birthright will last you a lifetime. I'm only going to be tasting this stew for a month or two!

JACOB: It's too late to change your mind.

ESAU: But I traded away something everlasting.

JACOB: So, you got what you wanted—a bowl of stew.

ESAU: And everlasting heartburn.

JACOB: It's not my fault you couldn't resist the temptation.

ESAU: And I can't change my mind?

JACOB: Too late for that!

ESAU: Well, in that case, dish me out another bowl . . . only this time, make it the laundry!

Noah and the Nosy Neighbor

The Story of Noah and the Ark

• A comedy sketch •

Props:

> A stepladder, short enough to be safe
> A waterproof canvas to lay on the floor*
> Two buckets of water, kept off-stage*

Characters:

> NOAH
> NEIGHBOR (not as tall as he is nosy!)

▼

(Scene opens with NOAH pantomiming working on the ark. The stepladder is off to the side, symbolizing the ramp up to the door of the ark. NOAH continues working as conversation ensues.)

NEIGHBOR *(approaching NOAH)*: Hey, pal! Whatcha building?

NOAH: An ark.

NEIGHBOR *(looks from the floor to ceiling, then looks back at NOAH, puzzled)*: An ark, huh? . . . Hope it has an elevator!

NOAH *(shakes head)*: Permit got rejected.

NEIGHBOR *(walking around, looking the ark over)*: So, tell me, why are you building this ark?

NOAH: God told me to.

---

*Since water is used as a prop in this sketch, it is not recommended to be performed in the sanctuary. A fellowship hall, youth center, or other area is suggested.

NEIGHBOR: God, huh? Is that the name of the building inspector?

NOAH: Not quite.

NEIGHBOR: Oh, God! Like in *(points heavenward)* . . . God!

NOAH: Yep.

NEIGHBOR: You talk to God, do you?

NOAH: Yep.

NEIGHBOR: And He tells you to build things?

NOAH: He told me to build this ark.

NEIGHBOR *(looking upward)*: So, why did it have to be so big? Did He get a deal on lumber or something?

NOAH: I don't know. He just wanted it big, I guess.

NEIGHBOR *(pretending to inspect the work)*: You ever build one of these before?

NOAH: No.

NEIGHBOR: Then how did you know what to do?

NOAH: Just followed directions.

NEIGHBOR: Oh, I get it! This is one of those kits.

NOAH: No, God told me what to do.

NEIGHBOR *(bored)*: Him again??

NOAH: Yep.

NEIGHBOR: But I don't understand. Why'd He want you to build an ark?

NOAH: He said He was going to be sending a flood.

NEIGHBOR: A flood? *(laughs)* And you believed Him?

NOAH: I'm building this ark, aren't I?

NEIGHBOR: Noah, you ol' fool! You probably just misunderstood Him!

NOAH: So, why take chances? Besides, I've ALWAYS obeyed God, and look where it's gotten me!

NEIGHBOR *(looks around laughing)*: You're building an ark in the middle of the desert! That's where it's gotten you!

NOAH *(confident):* It's going to rain. I know it is.

NEIGHBOR *(sarcastic):* Of course it is, Noah!

NOAH: You'll see!

NEIGHBOR *(pretending to feel side of ark):* Noah, Noah, Noah! You do good work! Give up this crazy notion and come over and panel my den!

NOAH: I don't have time. I've got to get the rest of the animals on board!

NEIGHBOR: You're taking animals?

NOAH *(matter-of-factly):* Two of each kind. God told me to.

NEIGHBOR *(sarcastic):* Sounds like a fun trip.

NOAH *(impatient):* Well, I'd love to stay and chat—but there's a couple of elephants waiting for me at the loading ramp.

NEIGHBOR *(laughs sarcastically):* What do you have to do? Check in their trunks? *(Laughs again.)*

NOAH *(ignoring the neighbor's sarcasm):* Something like that. You will excuse me then?

NEIGHBOR: Oh, sure. Go ahead and load all your *(clears throat)* passengers. I'll just wait here till you're finished.

NOAH: Suit yourself, but the clouds are starting to gather now. *(Starts walking away.)*

NEIGHBOR: Yeah, well, I still say your God is way off on this one, buddy!

NOAH *(holds hand out, then reacts is if a drop of rain just hit his hand):* That sure felt like rain to me.

NEIGHBOR: A drop here . . . a drop there—big deal! You're not going to scare me on board that ark!

NOAH: I really do have to go now. The elephants . . .

NEIGHBOR *(cuts in):* Oh, don't let me stop you! I'll just be waiting here when you decide to admit I'm right and unload everybody.

NOAH *(calmly):* You're getting pretty wet.

NEIGHBOR *(unyielding):* You call THIS wet?

NOAH: No. *(Bucket of water is thrown on NEIGHBOR from side of stage)* I call THAT wet!

NEIGHBOR: A few sprinkles. BIG DEAL!

(A second bucket of water is thrown on NEIGHBOR.*)*

NOAH: Still say it's not going to flood?

NEIGHBOR *(stubborn):* We could use a good rain.

NOAH *(starts to climb ladder):* Well, I really must be getting on board now.

NEIGHBOR: What's the matter, Noah? You afraid of a little water?

NOAH: A little? It's at your waist already!

NEIGHBOR: That doesn't mean anything. I'm short! And besides, this street doesn't have good drainage.

NOAH *(climbing up the ladder):* Well, the animals are all loaded. I guess I'll be getting on board myself.

NEIGHBOR *(pantomimes splashing water):* You don't know what you're missing, Noah! This is fantastic! If only I had a surfboard! Why, just look at all this water! Hey, I bet this is great fishing! I should go get my rowboat! . . . Imagine! Deep-sea fishing in my own backyard! And it's getting deeper by the minute. *(Swims around a bit)* Ouch! I think I just scraped my leg on someone's chimney. *(A little frightened)* Oh, Noah!

NOAH *(sitting on top of the stepladder):* Sorry, I don't mean to be rude, but I do have to close the door now.

NEIGHBOR: Well, that's what I wanted to talk to you about, buddy. How much would a cabin on that fine boat cost me, eh pal?

NOAH: Sorry, but all the rooms are taken. You should have made reservations.

NEIGHBOR: Well, hey, I don't mind bunking with a moose!

NOAH: Yeah, but THEY might complain.

NEIGHBOR: Well, how about if I stay with the giraffes? They won't mind. They've stuck their necks out for me before.

NOAH *(pretending to close the door):* I really do have to go now.

NEIGHBOR: Wait a minute, Noah! (NOAH *stops)* Now, there's no need to shut the door just yet. I mean, you're not sailing on schedule or anything, are you?

NOAH: From the way you're treading water there, I think I am. (NOAH *pretends to shut the door, then turns to sit on ladder with his back to the neighbor)*

NEIGHBOR: All right, Noah ... so I laughed at your silly ark! You don't have to take it so personal! I'M SORRY, OK? ... Boy! TOUCHY, TOUCHY, TOUCHY! *(Pause)* Hey! I said I was sorry! Noah? C'mon guy! Look, when you said a flood, I thought you meant a flood. I didn't know you meant a FLOOD! *(Pretending to tread water)* Besides, how was I supposed to know your God's so accurate with weather predictions? Noah? Noah, can you hear me? (NOAH *doesn't turn around)* All right, be that way! Leave me to drown! See if I care! *(Pause)* You wouldn't leave me here to drown, would you? Huh, Noah? Buddy? Pal? ... I'll be your best friend! Noah? *(Pause)* All right, I realize I had plenty of time to get on board, but let's just say your story bears so much more weight now that I'm out here treading water! Noah! Noah? ... Ohhh—it's no use! He can't hear me! *(Looks to left, then to right, then looks lost as he screams out in desperation)* Anybody seen the coast guard?

Who Said Animals Are Dumb?

The Story of Noah and the Ark

• A comedy sketch •

Characters:

ANIMAL NO. 1 (may be any kind of animal with fur)
ANIMAL NO. 2 (same type as ANIMAL NO. 1)

▼

(Scene opens with ANIMALS NOS. 1 *and 2 on the ark of safety . . . but they're not sure why.)*

ANIMAL NO. 1: Well, this is a fine mess you got me into!

ANIMAL NO. 2 *(defensive): I* got you into?? Look! I didn't tell you to follow me!

ANIMAL NO. 1: But, I thought you knew where you were going!

ANIMAL NO. 2: I never know where I'm going!

ANIMAL NO. 1: No argument there!

ANIMAL NO. 2: For the record . . . I was just following those two elephants in front of us.

ANIMAL NO. 1: You mean THOSE two elephants? *(Pointing)*

ANIMAL NO. 2: Of course those two elephants, lamebrain! Do you see any OTHER elephants?

ANIMAL NO. 1: No, just those two there. The rest of the herd was too smart to get on board this—this—what is this thing, anyway?

ANIMAL NO. 2: I think the old man calls it an ark.

ANIMAL NO. 1: An ark, huh? . . . Couldn't he take up another hobby? I mean, this could get awful expensive after a while!

ANIMAL NO. 2: I overheard the elephants saying that God told him to build this ark.

ANIMAL NO. 1: Now, why would God tell anyone to build an ark out here in the middle of a desert?

ANIMAL NO. 2: They said because it's going to rain.

ANIMAL NO. 1: So, couldn't the old man just get a raincoat like everyone else?

ANIMAL NO. 2: They say it's going to rain A LOT!

ANIMAL NO. 1: So—he gets boots, too.

ANIMAL NO. 2: According to the elephants, the old man thinks a flood's coming.

ANIMAL NO. 1: Face it, babe, the old guy's in La La Land, and the sooner we get off this floating looney farm, the better!

ANIMAL NO. 2: But the elephants . . .

ANIMAL NO. 1 *(cutting in)*: Oh, you can't believe everything an elephant says! I mean, sure, they never forget, but they're gullible—very gullible.

ANIMAL NO. 2: All right, then, what have you got to say about all the other animals? You know there's two of every kind on board this ark! They must believe in the old man's story.

ANIMAL NO. 1: Come here, I want to show you something. *(Walks over to imaginary window. Looks out.)* Does that look like rain to you? Why, there's not a cloud in the sky!

ANIMAL NO. 2: But I heard the weatherman forecast sunny skies. And you know that's *always* a sure sign it's going to rain!

ANIMAL NO. 1: Yes, my dear. You do have a point there. But, hey, it'd have to rain 40 days and 40 nights to float a boat this size!

ANIMAL NO. 2: Maybe it's going to.

ANIMAL NO. 1: Get serious! *(Looks out window again)* There's not a cloud in the . . . well, OK, there IS that one itty, bitty one way over there. But it's not even close.

ANIMAL NO. 2: Well, all I know is what I heard the elephants say.

ANIMAL NO. 1: You probably just misunderstood them. You know elephants—they talk through their noses.

ANIMAL NO. 2: You really don't believe it's going to rain, do you?

ANIMAL NO. 1: How could it? There's only *(looks out window again)* four or five medium-sized clouds in the sky. I'd hardly call that a storm.

ANIMAL NO. 2: Well, whatever. But, we're here now, so you might as well relax and enjoy it.

ANIMAL NO. 1 *(looks out at audience)*: I'm stuck on a boat in the middle of the desert, and she wants me to enjoy it. I mean, I've heard of budget cruises, but this is ridiculous!

ANIMAL NO. 2 *(sticks paw out window)*: It's starting to sprinkle.

ANIMAL NO. 1 *(looks out window)*: Big deal! What are we going to do—cruise a puddle?

ANIMAL NO. 2: Oh, I don't think we have to worry about that! *(Points to the sky)* Look at those clouds!

ANIMAL NO. 1: So what? There's not enough rain coming down to wash the sawdust off the old man's sandals!

ANIMAL NO. 2: Now there is! It's starting to pour!

ANIMAL NO. 1 *(takes another look out the window)*: OK, so it's starting to come down pretty hard now. We're still not floating off to sea!

ANIMAL NO. 2: Look, if you're so skeptical, why don't you go ahead and join all the others down there laughing at the old man and his silly boat? I mean, no one's forcing you to stay on board. So, go on! Jump off! I'll just go the rest of the cruise alone!

ANIMAL NO. 1: Well, now, there's no need to be hasty! And besides, my fur shrinks when it gets wet.

ANIMAL NO. 2: Oh, why don't you just admit it—you're glad the old man listened to God and built this ark.

ANIMAL NO. 1: Well, it IS keeping us dry.

ANIMAL NO. 2: You know, it took an awful lot of guts for him to build this ark. And an awful lot of faith.

ANIMAL NO. 1: It took guts all right!

ANIMAL NO. 2: I mean, those people really gave him a hard time!

ANIMAL No. 1: Maybe he's hard of hearing and couldn't hear everyone laughing at him.

ANIMAL No. 2: Oh, he heard. He just didn't let the ridicule stop him from obeying God. *(Grabs hold of imaginary rail)* Hey! I think we're starting to move!

ANIMAL No. 1: You're right. *(Looks a little seasick)* Oh boy, are you right!

ANIMAL No. 2: See? The old man knew what he was talking about, didn't he?

ANIMAL No. 1: I never doubted him for a moment.

ANIMAL No. 2: What?!!

ANIMAL No. 1: Now, aren't you glad you followed me onto this ark?

ANIMAL No. 2: I followed YOU? Wasn't it the other way around?

ANIMAL No. 1: OK then, you followed me. Is that better?

ANIMAL No. 2: Yeah . . . I think. *(Looks puzzled)* Oh well, who cares? It really doesn't matter as long as we're both safe. That's what's important.

ANIMAL No. 1: You know what really baffles me, though?

ANIMAL No. 2: What's that?

ANIMAL No. 1: Well, aside from the old man's family, the rest of the passengers on board are animals.

ANIMAL No. 2: Yeah, so?

ANIMAL No. 1: Well, if humans are supposed to be so smart, why aren't there more of them on board. I mean, let's face it. We are in the majority!

ANIMAL No. 2: You know, you're right!

ANIMAL No. 1: And to think they call US dumb animals!

ANIMAL No. 2: Yeah! *(Laughs sarcastically)* At least we know when to get in out of the rain!

A Lesson in Public Speaking

The Story of Moses

• A comedy monologue •

Character:

MOSES

▼

(MOSES *has just received the commission to go to Egypt and speak to Pharaoh. Appears with staff in hand.*)

OK, Lord, let me see if I've got this straight . . . You want me to go before Pharaoh and convince him to let Your people go—just like that? Me? Moses, who flunked public speaking in high school? You want ME to go talk to Pharaoh?

What's the matter with my brother, Aaron? He was on the debate team! Let him go!

What's that? . . . You say he CAN go, but I'm still the one You've chosen for the job?

Oh, now, don't get me wrong, Lord. I'm flattered . . . and I really do appreciate Your faith in me. It's just that I don't know if I can handle the job. I mean, what if Pharaoh doesn't WANT to let Your people go? What happens then? Have You thought about that? After all, Pharaoh isn't the most cooperative person in the world, You know. In fact, sometimes he can be pretty grouchy! Why, the last guy who told him to have a nice day is now dusting pyramids in the desert!

What's that? You say You've worked all of that out? . . . Well, OK, just as long as You know what You're . . . What? Oh, this? (*Looks at his staff*) . . . It's just my shepherd's staff. Yes, I guess it is pretty worn out. I've ordered a new one, but it's taking forever to get here. What's that? You want me to throw it down on the ground? . . . Well, all right, but I told You my new one isn't here yet. (*Throws down his staff*) . . . What? You want me to pick it up again ? . . . But I don't understand why You wanted

31

me to . . . (*Bends over to pick up staff*) YIKES! (*Jumps back in fear and amazement*) How'd You do that?!! . . . What do You mean, WHAT? That! (*Points to staff on the ground*) You turned my staff into a snake! (*Backing away from it*) You know I hate snakes, Lord!

What's that? You want ME to GRAB it by the TAIL? . . . You're kidding. . . . You're not kidding? . . . By the tail, huh? You mean THAT tail? (*Points*) The one that's getting ready to wrap itself around my left leg? . . . Just grab it by the tail, huh? . . . All right, that's what I'll do. (*Looks up, stalling*) I don't suppose You'd consider dropping a big rock on its head first, huh? (*Takes a deep breath*) Well, all right. I think I'm ready now . . . just let me get a little bit closer, then I'll grab it by the tail like You said. (*Creeping toward it*) After all, You're more powerful than this little ol' (*Grabs stick*) . . . stick? (*Looks at staff in amazement*) You turned that snake back into my staff again!

Hey! I'm impressed! So, this is how You're going to convince Pharaoh to let Your people go! (*Nods approvingly*) It should work.

What's that? You say there's more? You mean if Pharaoh doesn't cooperate You've got other ways to convince him? . . . I'm sure glad I'm on Your side!

Well, yes, I suppose that does mean I'm going to do it. . . . After all, if You've got that much faith in me, how can I have any less?

Yes, I'll go . . . and together we'll bring Pharaoh to his knees! I'll be the GREATEST spokesman You ever had! . . . And I'll even do it without cue cards!

A
Most Incredible
Battle

The Story of Gideon

• A comedy sketch •

Characters:

SCOOP MOSHAM (investigative reporter)
GIDEON
MAN

(Scene opens with SCOOP MOSHAM *trying to investigate the details of what just took place at the Midianite campsite.)*

SCOOP *(facing audience with microphone in his hand):* This is Scoop Mosham, reporting to you live from the Midianite campsite where the most incredible battle has just taken place. A small Israelite army has defeated the mighty Midianites! I repeat, the Midianites have just been defeated by what appears to have been only a handful of Israelite soldiers! . . . There's only one word for it, folks, and that's INCREDIBLE!

(To man walking by) Excuse me, sir, but could you tell us in your own words what happened here tonight?

MAN *(still in a daze):* Incredible!

SCOOP: You heard it yourself, folks! I said there was only one word to describe this battle, and that word is . . . *(holding microphone toward man)* . . .

MAN: . . . Incredible!

SCOOP (to audience): Let's see if we can't uncover a few more facts about this incredible battle. Stay with us as we attempt to interview the leader of this Israelite army . . . that is, if we can locate him. There is such a crowd here today! People have come from all over just to see the abandoned Midianite campsite. (GIDEON *walks by*) Excuse me, sir.

GIDEON (*stops and turns*): Yes?

SCOOP: Could you please tell me who it was who led the charge here tonight?

GIDEON: The Lord.

SCOOP: The Lord?

GIDEON: That's right.

SCOOP (*hesitates for a moment*): Well, then . . . who was second in command?

GIDEON: I suppose that would be me.

SCOOP: And you are . . . ?

GIDEON: Gideon.

SCOOP: Gideon, huh?

GIDEON: Yes.

SCOOP: Mind if I call you Giddy for short? (GIDEON *looks at him strangely.* SCOOP *clears his throat, then continues cautiously*) Well, uh, Gideon . . . I guess you're pretty overwhelmed with what took place here tonight, huh?

GIDEON: Not really. Actually, I EXPECTED to win.

SCOOP: You EXPECTED to defeat the Midianites?

GIDEON: Sure.

SCOOP: But, they had tens of thousands of men in their army! And how many did you say you had?

GIDEON: I didn't.

SCOOP: Well, someone said you only had 300.

GIDEON: Well, they were wrong.

SCOOP: You mean you had more than 300 in your army?

34

GIDEON: We had 301, counting God.

SCOOP: But what made you decide to go up against the Midianites with such a small army?

GIDEON: God was on our side.

SCOOP: But you had only 300 men!

GIDEON: We may have been small in number, but we were far more powerful!

SCOOP: You mean you had more sophisticated weaponry?

GIDEON: Sure! We had a trumpet, a pitcher, and a torch for each man.

SCOOP: A trumpet, a pitcher, and a torch? That's all?

GIDEON: Yep.

SCOOP: But you can't kill anybody with a trumpet.

GIDEON: Have you ever heard me play?

SCOOP: Well, what were the pitchers and torches for? Hot coffee?

GIDEON: God led our army, and those were the weapons he chose.

SCOOP: Personally, I think I would have gone AWOL.

GIDEON: We won, didn't we? . . . You know, we originally started out with 32,000 men!

SCOOP: Yeah, that's what I heard. What happened?

GIDEON: We didn't need them, so I sent them home.

SCOOP: You sent 31,700 men home?

GIDEON: Don't be ridiculous! I only sent 22,000 men home the first time.

SCOOP: But the Midianites had well over 32,000 men. Why would you want to send ANY of your army home?

GIDEON: God told me to.

SCOOP: He said, "Send 22,000 men home"?

GIDEON: No, He said to let everyone who was afraid go home.

SCOOP: And that just happened to be more than two-thirds of your army?

GIDEON: I guess.

SCOOP: Some army!

GIDEON: We won, didn't we?

SCOOP: Well, all right. But that left you with 10,000 men. What happened to the other 9,700?

GIDEON: They put their heads in the water to drink.

SCOOP: You sent them home for bad table manners?

GIDEON: No. You see, there was this brook, and God told me to watch the men as they drank from the water. Those who drank from their hands, keeping their eyes alert, would be my army. The others were to be sent home.

SCOOP: You sure run a strange draft, Gideon!

GIDEON: Just following orders.

SCOOP: So, after the brookside elimination, you were left with only 300 men?

GIDEON: You newsmen are such pessimists! I still had a nice little army. Why look at the negative all the time?

SCOOP: But 300 men against well over 32,000 Midianites. You didn't have a chance!

GIDEON: No! No! No! You've got it all wrong! It was the other way around.

SCOOP: What?

GIDEON: It was over 32,000 poor Midianites up against the mighty 300 soldiers of God! It was the poor unsuspecting Midianites who didn't have a chance.

SCOOP: Well, from the looks of this campsite, and the expressions on the faces of the Midianites as they ran past me headed toward the Jordan, I'd have to say you're quite right, Gideon. But tell me, where did the trumpets, the pitchers, and the torches come in?

GIDEON: All right, I'll tell you how we did it. . . . First of all, I divided my army into three groups.

SCOOP: One hundred in each, right?

GIDEON: Good guess! Then I gave each man a trumpet, a pitcher, and a torch.

SCOOP: Weird, but go on.

GIDEON: Then we all lit our torches and covered them with our pitchers.

SCOOP (*to audience*): I've heard some strange war stories in my time, but this one should win the Pulitzer!

GIDEON: Do you want to hear the story or not?

SCOOP: All right! I'll be quiet!

GIDEON: So, during the night we crept down the mountainside toward the Midianite camp, with each group taking their places on the sides of the camp.

SCOOP (*sarcastic*): All 300 of them?

GIDEON: You said you'd be quiet.

SCOOP: All right, so what happened then?

GIDEON: So, I blew loud on my trumpet . . .

SCOOP: And that's when the Midianites took off running?

GIDEON (*indignant*): I'm not THAT bad! . . . No, what happened was this: after I blew my trumpet, I hit my pitcher against a stone, breaking it so the torch would shine through the night. Then everyone else did the same thing with their trumpets and pitchers.

SCOOP: And the Midianites surrendered?

GIDEON: Not yet. Then we all shouted "THE SWORD OF THE LORD AND GIDEON!"

SCOOP: THEN the Midianites surrendered?

GIDEON: They didn't just surrender! They took off running in every direction!

SCOOP: They thought they were surrounded and didn't have a chance, huh?

GIDEON: You've got it.

SCOOP: That's pretty good strategy after all.

GIDEON: Well, if I've learned anything through all of this, I've learned that when God's on your side . . . you can never be outnumbered!

The Jericho Two-Step

The Story of Joshua and the Battle of Jericho

• A comedy sketch •

Characters:

MAN FROM JERICHO
VISITOR

▼

(Scene opens with MAN FROM JERICHO *surveying an imaginary wall which, earlier that day, had—how should we say it—tumbled down.* VISITOR *approaches.)*

VISITOR: My, my, my! What happened here?

MAN FROM JERICHO *(not looking up):* I don't want to talk about it.

VISITOR: Your wall fall down?

MAN FROM JERICHO *(sarcastic):* No, it's just taking a rest.

VISITOR *(surveying the damage):* So, how'd it happen.

MAN FROM JERICHO: I said I don't want to talk about it!

VISITOR: Suit yourself.

MAN FROM JERICHO *(pacing):* Do you realize what this is going to cost to rebuild?

VISITOR: Does it go around the entire city?

MAN FROM JERICHO: The entire city!

VISITOR: Nothing.

MAN FROM JERICHO *(puzzled):* What do you mean, nothing?

VISITOR: Can't rebuild it. All the bricklayers are on strike.

MAN FROM JERICHO (*sarcastic*): Terrific.

VISITOR: You still haven't told me what happened.

MAN FROM JERICHO: You really want to know?

VISITOR: Sure.

MAN FROM JERICHO: You won't believe it.

VISITOR: Try me.

MAN FROM JERICHO: All right, but don't say I didn't warn you. . . . You see, it was a normal day here in Jericho . . . not much happening. Of course, nothing much EVER happens in Jericho. I guess you could say we're sort of the speed bump of Canaan! Anyway, about seven days ago this guy named Joshua and his army starts circling our city.

VISITOR: Circling it?

MAN FROM JERICHO (*nodding*): Circling it. Once every day for six days!

VISITOR (*puzzled*): They didn't attack?

MAN FROM JERICHO (*emphatic*): They just circled it!

VISITOR: Once every day for six days?

MAN FROM JERICHO: You got it.

VISITOR: Isn't that kind of strange?

MAN FROM JERICHO: Well, that's what I thought, too. But when I tried to warn everybody, they said I was being paranoid.

VISITOR (*interested*): So, then what happened?

MAN FROM JERICHO: Well, this goes on for six days.

VISITOR: Yeah?

MAN FROM JERICHO: But this morning they do something different!

VISITOR: What's that?

MAN FROM JERICHO: They don't just circle the city one time!

VISITOR: No?

MAN FROM JERICHO: They don't just circle the city TWO times!

VISITOR: No?

MAN FROM JERICHO: They circled it SEVEN times! That's when I KNEW something was up. We NEVER had an army just walk around our walls SEVEN times like that. . . . Except, of course, that army from Og—but they've fought one too many battles without their helmets on, if you know what I mean.

VISITOR *(nods):* I've heard about them.

MAN FROM JERICHO: Anyway, so after this Joshua and his army march around our walls for the seventh time, these seven priests take out their ram-horn trumpets and start blasting away.

VISITOR: So, what did you do?

MAN FROM JERICHO: I covered my ears, of course! I'm not into heavy horn!

VISITOR: Well, then, what happened?

MAN FROM JERICHO: They blow those horns and their entire army gives a great shout . . . and the next thing I know we're having open house!

VISITOR *(looking around at the ruins):* But how did they knock the wall down?

MAN FROM JERICHO: Beats me. We've had earthquakes that didn't do this much damage!

VISITOR: Well, there must have been some kind of trick behind it. Walls don't fall down all by themselves, you know.

MAN FROM JERICHO: But, I watched them! They never laid a hand on it!

VISITOR: So, how do you explain it, then?

MAN FROM JERICHO: Well, I did overhear one of their men saying it was their God who was responsible.

VISITOR: Their God?

MAN FROM JERICHO: Yep.

VISITOR: Doesn't He like walls?

MAN FROM JERICHO: Apparently He didn't like ours.

VISITOR: So, then, what did this Joshua and his army do?

MAN FROM JERICHO: Why, they came in and slew everyone in Jericho.

VISITOR: But you escaped.

MAN FROM JERICHO: Well, you see, I don't actually live IN Jericho. . . . But I did do all my shopping there.

VISITOR: I guess you won't anymore.

MAN FROM JERICHO: Do you realize it took years to build this wall, and this God of Joshua knocks it down with a trumpet blast and a shout!

VISITOR: I sure wouldn't want to do battle with a God like that!

MAN FROM JERICHO (*nodding*): I know! I told them they should have stuck to fighting that army from Og!

Take a Little Off the Sides

The Story of Samson and Delilah

• A comedy sketch •

Characters:

> SAMSON
> DELILAH

Props:

> Large paper scissors hidden somewhere on DELILAH'S person
> Sofa

▼

(Scene opens with SAMSON *and* DELILAH *sitting on the sofa.* DELILAH *is playing coy with him.)*

DELILAH: Samson *(cuddling up to him)* . . . What's the secret of your strength?

SAMSON: You mean, beside Wheaties?

DELILAH *(backing away):* C'mon Sam! I'm serious ! *(Getting closer)* You're such a STRONG man . . . *(bats eyelashes)* and I DO LOVE STRONG MEN!

SAMSON: Delilah . . . you love ANY kind of man!

DELILAH *(thinks for a moment):* Well, yes—that's true. But, STRONG men in particular. *(Cuddling)* So, what is it? Diet? Exercise? Aerobics? What IS it that makes you so . . . *(feels his arm muscle)* . . . so STRONG?

SAMSON: My strength cometh from the Lord.

DELILAH (*unimpressed*): Yeah, yeah—I know. You've told me that already MANY, MANY, MANY times. (*Anxious*) But there's got to be more to it than that, Sammypoo! . . . After all, nobody is as strong as YOU.

SAMSON (*smiles shyly*): I know.

DELILAH (*determined*): So, what is it? (*Quickly softening her tone of voice*) I mean, what is it that makes you such a strong, strong man? (*Playing coy*) C'mon, you can tell little ol' Delilah your secret.

SAMSON: No, I can't, Delilah. You see, if I told you, then you'd tell your mother, and she'd tell her friends . . . and before you know it the whole world would know!

DELILAH (*rising to her feet, excited*): So, there IS a secret to your fabulous strength!

SAMSON: And it's going to STAY a secret (*gritting his teeth*) . . . dear.

DELILAH (*pouting*): Then, actually, Sammykins, what you're really telling me is that you don't love me.

SAMSON: Now, I didn't say that!

DELILAH: If you loved me, you wouldn't keep secrets from me.

SAMSON: Well, this is one secret I can't tell ANYBODY . . . not even you, Delilah.

DELILAH (*sitting back down next to him, batting her eyelashes*): Not even me?

SAMSON (*emphatic*): Not even you! . . . You see, Delilah, God's blessed me with this fabulous strength, and . . . well, if I were to tell you my secret, then I would be failing God.

DELILAH (*matter-of-factly*): So?

SAMSON: I can't do that. God has a special purpose for my strength.

DELILAH (*rises to her feet and walks away from him*): There are ways I can find out your secret!

SAMSON (*aggravated*): Drop it, Di!

DELILAH (*turns and walks toward him again*): But I CAN'T drop it, Samson! All my life nobody's ever trusted me with their secrets!

SAMSON: Well, doesn't that tell you something, Gossip Gums?

DELILAH (*defensive*): Who are you calling Gossip Gums?! I CAN KEEP A SECRET!

SAMSON: ARE YOU KIDDING?! If God wanted to send a message to the whole world, all He'd have to do is whisper it in your ear and tell you to keep it to yourself!

DELILAH *(offended)*: So, what you're saying is I have a big mouth.

SAMSON *(rises to his feet and walks toward her. He romantically touches her lips)*: You have a lovely mouth, Delilah. *(Looking deep into her eyes)* It's like a beautiful fragrant flower—THAT NEVER CLOSES!

DELILAH *(walks away)*: That's it! I'm walking!

SAMSON *(taking her hand and pulling her back)*: Look, Delilah . . . It's not that big of a deal! All you need to know is that I'm the strongest man in the world . . . and I love you! Isn't that enough?

DELILAH *(thinks for a moment)*: No! . . . I have to know your secret!

SAMSON: Well, how do I know I can trust you?

DELILAH *(raising her right hand)*: I promise I won't tell a soul . . . *(brief pause)* and neither will Mom!

SAMSON *(angry)*: Face it, Delilah! You just can't keep a secret!

DELILAH *(pouting)*: Well, it's plain to see you don't love me. So, good-bye!

SAMSON *(sincere)*: I love you.

DELILAH: No, you don't.

SAMSON: But I do.

DELILAH: But, you don't.

SAMSON *(cautious)*: All right, if I do tell you my secret, will you promise to marry me?

DELILAH *(hesitant)*: That's the bargain, huh?

SAMSON: You love me, don't you?

DELILAH: Oh, yeah . . . it's not that! It's just that, well . . . I kind of had a date tonight.

SAMSON: Then, I guess you'll never know my secret.

DELILAH: Oh, all right . . . I'll cancel the date and we'll get married instead. *(Overly anxious)* SO, WHAT'S YOUR SECRET?! . . . *(softening her tone)* . . . Sweetheart?

SAMSON: It's my hair.

DELILAH *(doesn't realize he has just told her his secret)*: I know. I've been meaning to talk to you about that. Don't you EVER get a haircut?

SAMSON: My hair's the secret of my strength.

DELILAH: Your hair?

SAMSON: Yes. When I was a child, God told my mother to never let a razor touch my head. And she obeyed.

DELILAH *(fondling his long locks)*: I just thought you were trying to be hip or something.

SAMSON: So, now that you know my secret, can we order the wedding invitations?

DELILAH: Sure, but first, Buster, you're getting a decent haircut! *(Pulls out giant paper scissors and chases him offstage.)*

Goliath— the Big Guy from Philistia

The Story of David and Goliath

• A comedy monologue •

Character:

GOLIATH (bigger, uglier, and meaner than your run-of-the-mill giant)

▼

(Scene opens with GOLIATH pacing anxiously on stage. He's light on his feet, and every so often he practices his punches.)

All right—who's it gonna be? I'm ready to fight, I tell you . . . I'm ready to fight! So who's it gonna be? *(Looking toward no one in particular in the audience)* You there! You look like a decent challenger. Why don't you stand up and let me look at you? C'mon, hurry up! . . . *(Embarrassed)* Oh, you *are* standing up?

Well, then, how about you there with a mustache? *(He blushes)* Oh, excuse me, madam! *(Starts pacing impatiently)* Well, c'mon, who's it going to be? I'm ready to fight . . . and I'm feelin' mean—REAL MEAN! Send me your strongest man! I'll pound him into the ground! I'll tear him limb from limb! I'll rip out his tongue and feed it to the ravens! . . . Nothing personal, mind you!

So, who's brave enough to step into the ring with me? Huh? *(Throws a few practice punches)* Just think of the story your widow could tell your children . . . and they could tell their children . . . and their children could tell their children! Why, the story of your bravery will live for years to come. Unfortunately, you won't. But hey, that's a small price to pay for fame!

So, c'mon, what are you waiting for? I'll even fight you with one hand tied behind my back. . . . I'll fight you blindfolded . . . I'll—*(looks to side of stage, annoyed; then looks back toward the audience)* Excuse me. *(Now looks back to the side of stage as if he's talking to someone)* Hey, kid, get off the stage! I'm trying to talk here! . . . What's that? . . . You say you want to fight me? *(Laughs)* Yeah, sure! *(Sarcastic)* I'll pencil you in for one round 10 years from today! Now, beat it, kid! You're in my spotlight!

(Looks back toward the audience) Ummm, where were we? *(Brief pause)* Oh, yeah—send me your biggest, your strongest, your meanest . . . your—*(looks over toward the side of stage once more; now he's quite irritated)* What IS it, kid? *(Brief pause)* OK, so you want to fight me! I SAID, come back when you've got all your permanent teeth, and I'll be happy to knock them all out for you! . . . Now, get lost! *(To audience)* Persistent little brat—I mean *(smiling)*, child, isn't he.

But, let's not waste our time on him. We've got more important matters to attend to. . . . So, c'mon, which one of you is feeling brave enough to take me on? Huh? *(Looks around impatiently)* Well, now, don't all of you come rushing up here at once!

Who's that, you say? David? *(Excited)* Well, all right! SEND HIM UP! *(Looks over audience)* Well? Where is he? *(Pause)* What do you mean he's up here already?

(To side of stage again, but this time GOLIATH *is even more irritated)* Hey, kid! You're beginning to get on my nerves! Now, I told you to get off the stage—so SCRAM! There's going to be a fight here, and I wouldn't want you to get hurt. *(Pause)* Oh, you want to know who's fighting? . . . Why, me and some dude named David. *(Pause)* Oh, your name's David, too, huh? *(Sarcastic)* Well, listen, David—I think I just heard your mother calling you!

What? . . . You say YOU'RE the David who's going to fight me? *(Laughs hysterically)* IN YOUR DREAMS, KID! . . . Look, I'm a giant! Giants don't fight squirts! . . . It's the old rule about picking on someone your own size. I mean, we do have our ethics!

(To audience) Israel! Is this the BEST you could do? YOU INSULT ME! . . . Take the kid home! It's time for his nap! *(To side of stage again)* Hey, what's that in your hand? . . . Oh, it's a slingshot, huh? *(Laughing to audience)* A giant fighting a kid with a slingshot! Boy! There's one for the history books!

(To side of stage) All right, kid, the joke's over! Take your slingshot and go home. You don't have a chance against me.

What's that? You say you're not fighting alone? . . . Your Lord is with you? *(Laughs)* Did He bring a slingshot, too? *(Laughs again)* Look, why don't you and your Lord go skim pebbles across the river and leave the giant-slaying to someone with the right kind of weapons! So, go on— scoot along home, little boy!

SAY! Watch where you swing that thing! Someone's liable to get hurt! . . . I SAID PUT THAT THING AWAY! . . . DID YOU HEAR ME?! *(Flinches)* OOOOOOUUUUUCCCCHHHHH! Look what you've done! You hit me right between the eyes! *(Stumbling)* And ooooooohhhhhh, have I got a headache! *(Barely standing up)* . . . Say, you and your Lord make a pretty good team! *(About ready to collapse)* Just do me one favor! . . . The next time I see you two together, remind me to pick on someone MY own size! (GOLIATH *collapses onto the floor.*)

A Whale of a Predicament

The Story of Jonah

• A comedy monologue •

Character:

JONAH

(Scene takes place inside the belly of a whale—imaginary, of course.)

(Cupping his hands over his mouth) Hey! Can anybody hear me? Hello! . . . Is anybody out there?

(Disgusted) Oh, it's no use! There isn't anyone within miles of here. And even if they could hear me, they'd probably think it's the whale . . . and who listens to whales???

(Looking around at the imaginary surroundings) Boy!! What a mess! This guy doesn't even chew his food! . . . And talk about BAD BREATH! No wonder he was traveling alone. *(Looks around again; then, as if he has just discovered something)* AHA! Just as I thought! This guy had scampi for dinner. I can still smell the garlic! . . . Now I know how my stomach feels every time I have pizza!

(Looks upward in disgust) Oh, no! Not again! *(Ducking)* All this guy does is eat! *(Cups his hands over his mouth and shouts upward)* Say, Buddy—there's no more room down here! *(Brushes himself off)* Hasn't he ever heard of Weight Watchers? *(Tries to lift leg to walk, but it won't budge)* Uuuggghhh! Gum! . . . Didn't your mother ever tell you NOT to swallow your gum? *(With some effort he pries his foot loose, disgusted)* All right, that does it! I'm getting out of here! I've just got to figure out my plan of escape. *(Planning)* Ummm . . . let's see . . . I could tap-dance on his cavities—but I guess that's hitting below the nerve. *(Thinks some more)* How about if I wait until he opens his mouth again, then try to swim out against the tide? *(Thinks about that for a moment)* Naw—that wouldn't

work. The way this guy sucks in water, I'll probably drown in the process! . . . I suppose I could give him an upset stomach by jumping up and down four or five hundred times . . . but I really don't think I'd like to see him get sick from this angle.

(Discouraged) Aw, I might as well face it. I'm stuck down here. Besides, I'm just getting what I deserve, I guess. After all, I have been running away from the Lord. *(Looks up)* But, hey, Lord, I didn't realize Nineveh meant so much to You! . . . I mean, Lord—it's a wicked city! A bunch of losers! Why waste Your time on them? They're NEVER going to repent of their sins. They're NEVER going to change! *(Pause as if God is talking to him)* Well, yes, Lord, I suppose I did repent of MY sins, but what . . . *(Another pause)* Well, yes . . . all right, I guess I did change. But, Lord, the people of Nineveh are DIFFERENT! Their sins are BAD, Lord . . . and we're talking about biggies here. (Another brief pause) Well, yes, I know a sin's a sin, but . . . *(Pause)* Well, yeah, I know there are no "little" sins, but . . . *(Impatient pause)* All right, look—we're not getting anywhere with this, so . . . here's what I propose: *(persuasive)* let me go to Egypt, Lord. I'll hold big tent meetings, crusades, revivals, Vacation Bible Schools—whatever You want. Wouldn't that be enough to make up for Nineveh? *(Pause)* No? Well, how about a big youth rally? We'll rent a pyramid—a vacant one, of course. Great acoustics! . . . Surely THAT would make You forget about Nineveh! *(Pause)* No, again, huh? BOY, WHEN YOU SET YOUR MIND TO SOMETHING . . . !

All right, so tell me, Lord, why is Nineveh so important to You? They've continually rejected You. They want no part of Your Word. So, why not forget about them? *(Pause, then answers impatiently)* But how COULD You love them?

(Looks up) Oh, no! *(Disgusted)* It's MEALTIME again! Where does this guy think he's at—a smorgasbord?!!? MAN THE BATTLE STATIONS— ONE ALL-YOU-CAN-EAT SUSHI BAR COMIN' DOWN!

(Brushing himself off) Whew! I sure hope that satisfies him for a while! . . . I'm beginning to feel like an after-dinner mint.

Now, where were we? . . . Oh, yeah . . . back to Nineveh! They're not worth the trouble, Lord—believe me! *(Pause)* So that's it, huh? You're not going to change Your mind? You love Nineveh and I'm the one who has to go tell them?

OK, Lord, let's look at my options. I can obey You and go to Nineveh, or I can stay here and try to make a life for myself inside this whale. *(Looks around, unimpressed)* There isn't a whole lot to do down here, Lord. I mean, I've already flossed his teeth—and played four choruses of Babaloo on his tonsils. And to tell You the truth, Lord, I don't think I want to stick around here for breakfast! And besides, *(sincere)* I really don't like running away from You! *(Looks around, disgusted)* I mean, look where it gets me! *(Pretends to be wading through all the food and garbage)* Nineveh can't be THIS bad!

(Brushing himself off) All right, Lord—I'll go to Nineveh, and I'LL GO WITH A SMILE! Just get me out of here, and fast!

(Looks upward) Hey! What's that? *(Listens)* . . . Sounds like this guy is trying to sneeze! *(Excited)* Now's my chance to break out of here . . . *(Coaxing whale)* Ah . . . ah . . . *(stops abruptly once more)* Oh, come on—sneeze already!! *(Coaxing even more enthusiastically)* Ah . . . ah . . . CHOO!!

(Pretends to be almost flying off stage as last line is shouted) God bless you—AND GOOD-BYE!! Nineveh—HERE I COME . . . A-I-R-M-A-I-L!!

What's All the Growling About?

The Story of Daniel and the Lions' Den

· A comedy sketch ·

Characters:

CORNELIUS
SIMEON
NARRATOR
CORNELIUS and SIMEON are two of the princes who sought the death of Daniel

▼

(Scene opens with CORNELIUS *and* SIMEON *watching from afar off as Daniel is being led to the lions' den.)*

CORNELIUS: Well, it worked!

SIMEON: Better than we could have imagined!

CORNELIUS *(laughs):* Did you see the look on Daniel's face when we told him about King Darius' new law?

SIMEON: You mean OUR new law, don't you? WE tricked the king into signing that stupid ordinance just like we tricked him into signing all the other ordinances over the years!

CORNELIUS: Yeah, like the one that says it's illegal to paint sheep. *(Laughs.)*

SIMEON *(surprised):* Is THAT on the the books?

CORNELIUS: Of course. Don't you remember?

SIMEON *(sighs):* Well! There goes my Saturday nights!

CORNELIUS (*looks at him strangely*): You know, sometimes, Simeon, I don't think your chariot's riding on both wheels!

SIMEON (*sincere*): Thank you.

CORNELIUS (*puzzled*): Well, anyway . . . you know, I figured if we appealed to Darius' vanity streak, he'd sign that decree forbidding anyone to bow down before any other king for 30 days.

SIMEON: Yeah, but Darius didn't realize that ordinance he signed was also Daniel's death warrant!

CORNELIUS: Oh, please, my strange little friend. Don't call it a death warrant. That's such an ugly term. . . . Just say we're giving Daniel the opportunity to embark upon a new career—as a lion-tamer!

SIMEON (*laughs fiendishly*): Sort of on-the-job training, eh?

CORNELIUS: Of course. I just hope it doesn't take too much out of him, if you know what I mean.

SIMEON: Like demanding he be in two places at once?

CORNELIUS: Or three or four.

SIMEON: Or five or six.

CORNELIUS: You realize, of course, there is the distinct possibility that Daniel will go completely to pieces under the pressure of his new job.

SIMEON: Isn't that the idea?

CORNELIUS: I'm just glad he's finally out of our hair. Personally I was getting rather tired of his rotten attitude.

SIMEON: Rotten attitude? Daniel? All he ever did was smile!

CORNELIUS: I know. That's what I mean. Why couldn't he be miserable like the rest of us?

SIMEON: I didn't like him because he always acted as though he was the right hand of Darius.

CORNELIUS: Well, that was his official title.

SIMEON: So—Darius is left-handed! And besides, what did King Darius need with someone like Daniel? I mean, efficiency can get old after a while!

CORNELIUS: Well, anyway, we won't have to compete with Mr. Perfection anymore. He's broken the law, and now he is going to pay!

SIMEON: Lucky for us we caught him praying!

CORNELIUS: Luck had nothing to do with it, Simeon! That fanatic goes to the very same window three times every single day at the very same time every single day, and prays with the same fervency every single day. You could set your sundial to him!

SIMEON: Well, let's see his prayers save him now!

CORNELIUS: Tell me, Simeon, are the lions hungry?

SIMEON: They haven't been fed for a week!

CORNELIUS: Good! I can't stand to watch a lion just pick at his dinner! Especially when we've gone to this much trouble to serve it to him!

SIMEON: You won't have to worry about that! In fact, I can hear them smacking their lips from here!

CORNELIUS: That's not the lions, you idiot! That's the guy in the seat behind us eating popcorn! . . . Look! Darius is giving the signal . . . it's time!

SIMEON: Poor old Darius. He doesn't even realize he was tricked into having his best friend killed.

CORNELIUS: Farewell, Daniel . . . Oh, yes—have a nice day!

SIMEON: There he goes! They've dropped him into the den!

CORNELIUS: I can't look! I have a weak stomach.

SIMEON: Then why are you taking pictures?

CORNELIUS: They're just sketches. I'm drawing them for my scrapbook. I'd like to remember Daniel as he was . . . you know . . . before he fell apart.

SIMEON: Well, you'd better hurry up and finish. The soldiers are getting ready to cover the den with a large stone.

CORNELIUS: What?

SIMEON: And look! King Darius is sealing it with his signet. I guess he doesn't want to watch.

CORNELIUS: Well, I do . . . Now what do they expect us to do for entertainment?

SIMEON: Have you ever tried painting sheep?

CORNELIUS: It could never be as much fun as watching Daniel bite the dust!

SIMEON (*thinks for a moment*): No, but it's a real close second!

CORNELIUS: Well, even if they don't let us watch it, it still feels good to know that we're finally rid of Goody-Two-Sandals once and for all!

SIMEON: Yeah. No one's ever survived the lions' den before!

CORNELIUS: Still, I would have enjoyed watching it.

SIMEON: You're not the only one!

CORNELIUS: So, what do you want to do now? Go home, or hang around here till morning?

SIMEON: Why don't we stay here? After all, if I can't paint sheep anymore, what else is there to do?

NARRATOR: And so these two men spent the night watching the lions' den and listening for any sounds of a struggle. But the night passed ever so quietly, and by morning, the two men were completely baffled!

CORNELIUS: I didn't hear a thing all night! How about you?

SIMEON: The only growling I heard was my stomach.

CORNELIUS: I thought you said those lions were famished!

SIMEON: They were! If you don't believe me, ask the den-keeper.

CORNELIUS: You mean Three-fingers Jerod?

SIMEON: No, I mean Two-fingers Jerod.

CORNELIUS: Look! I see King Darius coming now!

SIMEON: He ordering the stone to be removed.

CORNELIUS (*pause*): He's shouting something into the den. Listen!

SIMEON: Can you make out what he's saying?

CORNELIUS: Shhh!

SIMEON (*brief pause*): Well, what's he saying?

CORNELIUS: Shh!

SIMEON (*brief pause again*): Well? Can you hear what he's saying, Cornelius?

CORNELIUS: No! I can only hear what YOU'RE saying. Now be quiet! (Listens for a moment) He's saying, "Daniel, O Daniel, servant of the living God."

SIMEON: But, why is he talking to Daniel? Daniel's dead.

CORNELIUS: Poor man. He must be delirious with grief.

SIMEON: What's he saying now?

CORNELIUS: Shhh. (Listens for a moment.)

SIMEON: Well? What'd he say?

CORNELIUS (irritated): Are we going to go through this again?

SIMEON: I'll be quiet.

CORNELIUS (listens): He's saying, "Is thy God whom thou servest continually able to deliver thee from the lions?"

SIMEON: Darius just isn't giving up, is he?

CORNELIUS: Pitiful, isn't it. I mean, does he REALLY believe Daniel's God could have saved him from those ferocious lions?!!?

SIMEON: Wait! . . . Did you just hear someone say, "O King, live forever"?

CORNELIUS: It was probably Darius. He talks to himself a lot, you know.

SIMEON: But, it sounded like Daniel's voice!

CORNELIUS: Ridiculous!

SIMEON: It came from inside the den!

CORNELIUS: So? Maybe one of the lions is a ventriloquist.

SIMEON: Wait a minute! LOOK! Down there! . . . Isn't that Daniel?

CORNELIUS: It can't be Daniel. That man's in one piece!

SIMEON: Well, it IS Daniel! And look! His clothes aren't even ripped! In fact, he looks like he got a better night's sleep than we did!

CORNELIUS: You're right! It IS Daniel! . . . I recognize the smile. Doesn't ANYTHING ever depress that guy?

SIMEON: Uh-oh! The guards have spotted us!

CORNELIUS: What do we do now?

SIMEON: I don't know, but we'd better think of something quick. Darius doesn't look too happy!

CORNELIUS: I know. He's ordering the guards to throw all the conspirators against Daniel into the lions' den.

SIMEON: How do you know that?

CORNELIUS: He just said, "Throw all the conspirators against Daniel into the lions' den!"

SIMEON: Do you think he means us?

CORNELIUS: Well, I seriously doubt if the guards are walking over here to shake our hands. (CORNELIUS and SIMEON *struggle with imaginary guards.*) Hey! Wait a minute, you guys! It was just a joke! We knew Daniel's God would save him!

SIMEON: Yeah! (*Looks at* CORNELIUS) We did?

CORNELIUS: Sure! We just wanted to prove to King Darius that Daniel's God is the only TRUE God!

SIMEON: Yeah! (*Looks at* CORNELIUS) We did?

CORNELIUS: Yeah! It was all part of our plan!

SIMEON (*looks at* CORNELIUS): It was?

CORNELIUS (*being pushed offstage by imaginary guard*): Hey! C'mon, don't you believe me?

SIMEON (*also being pushed by imaginary guard*): Well, Cornelius, look at it this way, Daniel survived the lions' den.

CORNELIUS: I know, but he had his God with him! All I've got is YOU! (*Looks at audience*) And I've NEVER felt so ALONE in my entire life! (*To imaginary guard who's pushing him*) All right! I'm going, I'm going! (CORNELIUS *and* SIMEON *exit stage struggling with imaginary guards.*)

Pen Pals

The Story of the Prodigal Son

• A comedy monologue •

Character:

THE PRODIGAL SON

▼

(Scene opens with the PRODIGAL SON *speaking to us from the pig pen—wearing most of it!)*

Ah! This is the life! . . . OK, sure—this isn't exactly the Jerusalem Hilton. In fact, you're probably thinking it looks an awful lot like a pig-pen. But, hey, it's not any worse than a lot of teenagers' rooms I've seen! . . . And besides, here I don't have to answer to ANYONE! Not my dad, not my brother, not ANYONE!

Sure, I'll admit things didn't turn out quite like I expected them to. But, you see, I've had a few financial setbacks since leaving home . . . I've made some bad investments, made a lot of bad loans to my friends, and basically squandered most of my money.

Still, I don't think I've done too bad for myself. After all, I've got all the food I could possibly want to eat right at my fingertips . . . Actually *(looks a little disgusted)* I guess I should say it's down by my feet, oozing up between my toes! Nobody uses a plate here! It's like a smorgasbord without the board . . . a walk-through casserole . . . a slip-n-slide salad bar! They don't serve leftovers here—they wear them!

I've been trying to teach these pigs some manners, but it's no use. I give them napkins . . . and they eat them! I tell them to keep their elbows off the table . . . and they put their feet there instead! And I don't care if they snort till they're blue in the face, I still say gravy isn't a finger food!

But then, I guess that's a small price to pay for independence. You know, the right to do my own thing. And besides, I can't complain about my room. It's airy and bright . . . and I even have my own waterbed—that is, when the pigs let me sleep in the trough!

And talk about a view! Nothing but rolling hills and green grass for as far as the eye can see! Yes, sir! This is the life! I'm free to do what I want, go where I want, and be what I want. I don't have to answer to ANYBODY!

If I don't want to do my homework, nobody cares! You think a pig has to worry about computer skills?

If I don't want to clean my room, you think a pig's going to complain? No! In fact, they compliment it! The dirtier the better—that's their motto. And we're talking GRIME here. I mean, a pig is a connoisseur of dirt!

And best of all, there's none of that "Finish your dinner or you're going to bed" sermonizing! Hey, if I don't eat all of my food, do you think one of these pigs is going to care? Of course not! It just means more food for them to eat . . . or frolic in! Believe me, this is the life! No homework, no housework, no hassles! Nobody cares what I do here! It's as simple as that! Nobody cares.

(Thinks for a moment, then lowers his head and laughs sarcastically) I guess it's as simple as that—nobody does care.

(Growing more solemn) Oh, who am I kidding? This place is the pits, the end of the road, the bottom of the barrel! There's nothing for me here. I've no friends, no family, no future! . . . And mud isn't even my color!

You know, when I first left home, I had lots of friends. Of course, I had lots of money, too. But when the money disappeared, so did my so-called friends. Now the only friends I have are these pigs, and I don't even think they like me that much!

I've thought about going home. Why, the servants at my father's house live better than this! But after the fool I've made of myself, I wouldn't blame him if he never wanted to see me again!

Still, even if he doesn't welcome me home with open arms *(takes a whiff of his clothes)* and I can't say I blame him . . . maybe he'd let me work as his servant, at least. After all, I AM pretty good with pigs, you know.

Anyway, I've learned my lesson, and I'm ready to ask my father's forgiveness. I know now the world's happiness is shallow and temporary. The only true joy I had was in my father's house!

Yep! That settles it. I'm cleaning up my act and going home! . . . I broke my father's heart when I left home so long ago. I just hope it's not too late to say I'm sorry.

So, pigs—I'm giving you my notice! This boy's moving out and going home where he belongs!

(Starts to walk away whistling, then stops abruptly) I wonder if I should send a message on ahead to tell everyone I'm coming home? *(Thinks for a moment, then takes a good whiff of his clothing)* Naw! Why bother? They'll smell me! *(Walks offstage, whistling happily.)*

Just a Little Determination

The Story of Zacchaeus

• A comedy monologue •

Character:

ZACCHAEUS, a small man with big ideas

▼

(Opens with ZACCHAEUS moving through an imaginary crowd, jumping up and down trying to see over the heads of the people.)

Excuse me . . . Excuse me . . . If only I could get a little closer. Pardon me, but I can't see over . . . Oh, why'd I have to get stuck behind a Pharisee! I can't see anything at all through all of that headgear!

(Moves on, trying to make his way through the crowd) All I want to do is get a glimpse of Him! . . . Please, can I get through? *(Making his way through the crowd)* Excuse me. Pardon me. *(Stops short—no pun intended—and sighs in aggravation)* Oh, great! Now I get stuck behind a seven-foot Goliath! Isn't anybody in Jericho short besides me?

(Looks up and down surveying the size of this imaginary giant, then speaks) Excuse me, sir. Sir? Down here, sir! *(Tugs on what would be the giant's shirttail)* Sir, do you think you could move over just a wee bit? . . . Well, no, you don't have to if you don't want to. I just thought . . . You are? The heavyweight champion of Jericho, huh? . . . Oh, well, in that case, please don't bother. I'll just go find someone else's knees to stare into.

What's that? You're challenging ME to a fight? Oh, but, sir—I'm no fighter! The only time I ever step into the ring is when I collect taxes from the winner . . . and even then I get bruises from the ropes!

Yeah, I'm a tax man. Why? Oh . . . you say you don't like tax men? *(Nervously backing away)* Well, now, wait a minute, sir. It's only a job. I mean, somebody's got to do it! Sir—there's smoke coming out of your ears! (*Backs away some more*) Sir, would it help if I said it was only part time? In fact, I'm hardly EVER at the office! ... You shouldn't point with your sword, sir. (*Backing away even more*) Anyway, I really MUST be going. It was so nice to have met you—and do have a nice day!

(*Ducking in and out of the imaginary crowd,* ZACCHAEUS *quickly moves on. When he's sure he's lost him, he stops and pants.*)

Whew! I finally lost him! I guess that's one advantage to being short! And NOW for the advantage of being a tax man! (ZACCHAEUS *pulls out a small notebook from his pocket and makes a notation.*) That big bully's getting audited!!

In fact, if I don't get through to see Jesus pretty soon, I'm going to audit the whole city!

(*Starts making his way through the crowd again*) Excuse me. Excuse me. Can I get through? No? ... Is that "N" as in "Noah," ... "O"? No? Is that what you said? ... Very well, then, can I have your name? (ZACCHAEUS *makes another notation in his notebook*) Thank you! (*Starts to walk away, then turns back and shouts*) I hope you saved your receipts!

(ZACCHAEUS *moves on*) Pardon me. Can I get through here? ... No? Very well. Your name, please? (ZACCHAEUS *writes it down in his notebook*) Thank you. (*Moving on to the next person*) Excuse me. (*Clears his throat to get the man's attention*) Pardon me! ... Ah ha! You're one of the ones who wouldn't let me through before! ... Your name, please! (ZACCHAEUS *jots it down*) Thank you. (*Tries in vain to get through next group of people*)

Oh, this is ridiculous! (*Puts notebook away*) There must be SOME way I can get to see Jesus! All I want is a glimpse of this man I've heard so much about! I mean, I'm not dressed up enough to actually meet Him or anything. I just want a quick look.

(*Looks around*) Ummmm ... there's a tree over there ... I wonder ... I haven't climbed a tree since ... ummmm ... I don't think I've EVER climbed a tree. Not that people haven't tried their best to get me to! They're always saying, "Zacchaeus, why don't you go climb a tree?" (*Looks at audience*) Tax collectors don't have many friends, you know.

Let's see—that tree looks simple enough to climb. If I could just reach that bottom branch.

(ZACCHAEUS *tries to reach imaginary branch, but fails. He tries again, and he fails again*) Oh, why didn't God make ladders on these things!

(*He tries for the branch one more time, but this time he makes it; then struggles to climb on up*) There, I think I've got it! (*Looks out over the crowd*) Oh, yes, this is MUCH better! There's Jesus over there! (*Strains to get a good view of Jesus*) But I still can't get a good look at His face. Jesus! Look over here, Jesus! Up here in this tree! Jesus! (*Stretches his neck trying to get as good a look as possible, then sighs*) ... Oh, it's no use! He's NEVER going to look up here! Maybe He IS like all the others! I mean, after I go to all the trouble of climbing up in this stupid sycamore tree just to get a glimpse of Him, He doesn't even bother to look in my direction!

Oh, well, what's the use? I guess I'm just a bad investment on the 10-40 of life. I think I'll climb down and go home. *(He starts to climb down)* Hey, wait a minute! Did I hear someone calling my name? *(Looks around)* Yes? Yes? I'm up here . . . in this tree! *(Looks around again)* Yoohoo! Up here! *(Listens)* There they go again! And they're calling me by my REAL name instead of my nickname, "Hey you!"

(Looks around, then gasps in amazement) Why, it's Jesus! And He's looking right at me! *(Nervously)* Oh, my goodness! He's walking over here! I KNEW I should have dressed up today! . . . You ALWAYS meet somebody important when you look your worst!

Oh, well, maybe He won't care. *(Straightens himself up a bit. Brushes his clothing off with his hands, etc.)* Here He comes now! . . . Just look how everyone is staring! They're probably wondering why someone as important as Jesus Christ would waste His time with little ol' Short Form Zacchaeus! . . . As a matter of fact, I'm wondering that, too. After all, I'm usually the LAST person people want to see!

(Looks down) Yes, Jesus! . . . My name IS Zacchaeus. What's that? You say You'd like to come to MY house for dinner? . . . Are You SURE You don't have me mixed up with someone else? I mean, like someone more popular, more likable, more—well, how should I put it? . . . TALLER?

Oh, no, Jesus, don't get me wrong! Of course you're welcome! It's just that I'm not used to anyone wanting to be MY friend—except, of course, during an audit.

But look, if You REALLY do want to come to my house, I promise I'll fix You a feast like You've never had before! Just give me a minute to climb down from this tree. (ZACCHAEUS *climbs down from imaginary tree. As he does so, he mumbles to himself)* Just look at them stare . . . all those people who used to laugh at me because I'm short. They're not laughing now! That's because Jesus itemized my potential—computed the returns, so to speak. He saw the value of the person I'm capable of becoming, and not just my current net worth. He looked beyond my size, and saw the heights I could reach! So, I guess I'm not as small and insignificant as I thought! I guess I AM important to the kingdom of God.

(Walking away proudly) Come on, Jesus! Let's go have dinner!

The Very First All-You-Can-Eat Fish Fry

The Story of the Five Loaves and Two Fishes

• A comedy sketch •

Characters:

> PETER
> JOHN
> ANDREW
> MATTHEW

(Scene opens with PETER *sitting on a rock, tree stump, or other reasonable facsimile.* JOHN *and* ANDREW *are busy cleaning up after the big dinner.*)

PETER (*groaning*): Ohhhhhh, I can hardly breathe! I knew I should have passed on that last serving of fish! . . . And to think all that came from one little boy's lunch!

ANDREW: It was a miracle, brothers! A true miracle!

JOHN: You want some more fish, Peter? There's plenty left over!

PETER: Are you kidding?! I'm so full now that you guys are going to have to roll me back to the boat! Ohhhhh . . . (*holds stomach*)!

ANDREW: Nobody told you to eat a whole basket of fish yourself!

PETER: I know, but you know what smorgasbords are like. Your eyes are always bigger than your stomach.

JOHN: Can you believe what happened here today? Jesus fed a crowd of 5,000 men from one little boy's lunch of just five loaves and two fishes! And we still have 12 baskets leftover!

ANDREW: See if the people want seconds.

JOHN: Seconds?! They've already had thirds and fourths!

PETER: Well, don't look at me! I already feel like the whale that swallowed Jonah!

JOHN: This was quite a feast, wasn't it, Peter?

PETER: It was a miracle supper!

ANDREW: You know a lot of kids would have gone off and ate their lunch by themselves!

PETER: A lot of adults would have, too!

ANDREW: But because of this child's willingness to give what little he had, Jesus blessed and multiplied that so everyone got to eat!

PETER: And eat! And eat! And eat!

MATTHEW (approaches the others with basket of fish in his hands): More fish anyone! (JOHN, ANDREW, and PETER groan) There's plenty left over!

PETER: One more bite and you guys will be using me for an anchor!

ANDREW: That goes for me, too!

JOHN (groans): Ditto!

MATTHEW: It's been quite a day, hasn't it, my brothers?

ANDREW: That it has, Matthew! That it has!

PETER: Who would have thought we'd ever witness such a miracle?

JOHN: Well, I've learned one thing for sure!

ANDREW: What's that?

JOHN: I've learned to trust Him!

MATTHEW: We all have, John!

JOHN: After all, if He could feed a crowd of 5,000 men with just five loaves and two fishes, then He can surely meet our every need!

ANDREW: And then some! Don't forget there were women and children here, too! So, actually, Jesus fed more than 5,000.

MATTHEW: Plus we've got to take into consideration Peter's appetite!

JOHN: And we STILL had 12 baskets left over. So, there's no need for us to worry about tomorrow! All we've got to do is trust in Him!

ANDREW: Like the Psalmist said of old, "I've not seen the righteous forsaken nor his seed begging bread!"

PETER: And with Jesus it's ALWAYS an all-you-can-eat affair!

Mrs. Clean

The Story of Martha

• A comedy sketch •

Characters:

> MARTHA
> MARY

▼

(Scene opens MARTHA *holding a pile of dishes in one hand and a pitcher in the other.* MARY *is standing nearby.)*

MARTHA: Mary! Are you going to help me serve our guests or not?

MARY: I will, but first there are things I must do.

MARTHA: Like serve the drinks! *(Hands her the pitcher)* Now, get busy!

MARY: But I want to be with Jesus!

MARTHA: So do I. But first lets get our work done, Mary. There are guests to serve, dishes to wash, floors to sweep! There's LOTS to be done, Mary!

MARY: But all you ever think about is housework! Martha, don't you realize Jesus won't always be with us? Housework will always be here!

MARTHA: The way you do it, it will be! Don't you think Jesus appreciates a clean house and good food?

MARY: Of course. But first I want to tell Him how much I love Him by anointing His head and feet with fine perfume.

MARTHA: I prefer offering Him a clean place to sit down.

MARY: But Martha, Jesus needs to hear you say you love Him, too.

MARTHA: Jesus knows I love Him.

66

MARY: He still needs to hear you say it. That's why I bought this expensive perfume to anoint Him.

MARTHA: But what about our guests? They need to be served—and the house needs to be cleaned.

MARY: I'll help you later. I promise. *(Exits)*

MARTHA *(starts sweeping)*: I suppose I should go with Mary to tell Jesus I love Him, but I've so many things to do here first. I've got to finish serving the guests, then there's the cleanup—and I've got three loads of laundry to do . . . and there's a pile of dishes that have been soaking in the sink so long they've probably rusted by now. I just can't afford to take any time off. Not yet, anyway.

MARY *(reenters)*: Well, Martha. Are you coming with me, or not?

MARTHA: I'd love to, Mary. I really would. But I just don't have the time today.

MARY: I said I'd help you when we get back. Let's go be with Jesus a while; then we'll come back and do all this.

MARTHA *(sighs)*: Well, all right. But you go ahead. I'll be there just as soon as I finish sweeping.

MARY: OK. *(Starts to exit)*

MARTHA: I'll just finish sweeping; then I'll wash that pile of dishes in the sink . . . then I'll join you.

MARY: Great! *(Tries to exit again)*

MARTHA: It won't take me but a few minutes to finish this sweeping, wash that pile of dishes, and serve dessert. So, you go on ahead. I'll be right behind you!

MARY *(growing a little impatient)*: All right! *(Starts to exit once more)*

MARTHA: I'll just finish sweeping, wash that pile of dishes, serve dessert, and then put in a load of laundry to soak. It won't take me long at all.

MARY *(irritated)*: Well, for goodness sakes, Martha, why don't you just go ahead and clean the whole house?!!

MARTHA: What? And make Jesus wait?!! I WOULDN'T THINK OF IT!!

The Original Superhero

The Story of the Good Samaritan

• A comedy sketch •

Characters:

> SCOOP MOSHEN III (investigative reporter)
> INJURED MAN
> PRIEST
> LEVITE
> GOOD SAMARITAN

▼

(Scene opens with INJURED MAN *lying on the side of the road.* SCOOP MO-SHEN III *is there covering the story.)*

SCOOP: This is Scoop Moshen III reporting for the Jericho Daily News. We are here today by the side of the road where a man has been severely beaten, robbed, and left here to die. As usual, we were here to film it. The interesting thing, however, is that nobody has stopped to help this man. (PRIEST, *dressed in priest's apparel from that era, approaches)* Here, I'll show you what I mean. *(To* PRIEST) Excuse me, your holiness.

PRIEST: Yes?

SCOOP: I couldn't help but notice that you're walking on the far side of the road. Is there any reason for this?

PRIEST: Of course. There's a bleeding body over there *(points)*.

SCOOP: But aren't you going to help him?

PRIEST: Aren't you?

SCOOP: I'm on duty right now.

PRIEST: And I'm late for an appointment! (PRIEST *exits.*)

SCOOP *(to audience):* See what I mean? No one wants to help this poor man. Wait a minute! Here comes a Levite. Maybe he'll help. *(To* LEVITE) Excuse me, sir?

LEVITE: Yes?

SCOOP: Do you see the man over there?

LEVITE: You mean the one dying by the side of the road?

SCOOP: That's the one.

LEVITE: Yes, I see him.

SCOOP: Well, aren't you going to help him?

LEVITE *(looks toward the* INJURED MAN, *then looks back toward* SCOOP. *Says nonchalantly)* No.

SCOOP: No?

LEVITE: I'm not a doctor.

SCOOP: No, but perhaps you could help.

LEVITE: Perhaps YOU could help.

SCOOP: But I AM helping. I'm reporting the incident!

LEVITE: And I'm helping, too, by staying over here. I'm giving him air—plenty of air!

SCOOP: I think he needs more than air, sir.

LEVITE: Well, I'm sorry, but my policy is "NEVER GET INVOLVED!"

SCOOP: But what if that were your brother over there dying by the side of the road. Wouldn't you want someone to help him?

LEVITE: I suppose you're right. *(Walks over to wounded man, looks him over)* But he's NOT my brother. *(Exits)*

SCOOP *(to audience, pondering):* ". . . Not my brother . . ." Well, that about sums it up, doesn't it, folks? *(Pause)* Have we really become such a cold and callous society that a human life means so little to us? A man is beaten and robbed and left by the side of the road to die—and virtually no one is willing to help him.

(GOOD SAMARITAN *approaches.*)

GOOD SAMARITAN: What's going on here?

SCOOP: That man over there was beaten and robbed by thieves.

GOOD SAMARITAN: Is he all right?

SCOOP: He's probably going to die.

GOOD SAMARITAN: Hasn't anybody offered to help him?

SCOOP: No, they just walk by as if he's not even there.

GOOD SAMARITAN: Well, he won't die if I can help it.

SCOOP: I take it you know the man.

GOOD SAMARITAN: Do I have to know someone in order to help him?

SCOOP: It seems on this road you do.

GOOD SAMARITAN: Well, I have oil and bandages for his wounds. I'll do everything I can.

SCOOP: But aren't you a Samaritan?

GOOD SAMARITAN: Yes.

SCOOP: But this man is a Jew. I didn't think you guys got along.

GOOD SAMARITAN: This man's a brother—and he has a need. That's all that matters.

SCOOP (*to audience while the* GOOD SAMARITAN *goes over and helps the* INJURED MAN): If only we'd all act more like this good Samaritan, what a better world this would be!
And that concludes our broadcast. This is Scoop Moshen III signing off and saying—WHO SAYS WE DON'T REPORT THE GOOD NEWS?!

Learn the basics of play production for fellowship and outreach.

CREATE A DRAMA MINISTRY
By PAUL M. MILLER and DAN DUNLOP

There are very few ministry books that have had the amount of "field testing" that **CREATE A DRAMA MINISTRY** has had. Authors Miller and Dunlop have directed a local church drama program that has utilized most of the information presented. During this time, they have developed the philosophy of outreach drama that is spelled out in this book.

In seven chapters the reader is given a fast survey of how drama began in the church, what ministry is all about, and the special opportunities worship leaders have to use some form of drama in church worship services. From there, the book becomes a practical handbook that details the duties of the play director; how to choose a play script and conduct rehearsals; getting the most out of acting talent; handling the details of scenery, lighting, makeup, and costumes. The final chapter is a step-by-step guide to producing dinner drama—the particular method of outreach drama used by the authors. The book also contains a full appendix section that provides lists of publishers, suppliers, and sources for information. Also included is a glossary of stage terms and a reader's theatre scripting of Daniel 3, the story of the three Hebrew children and the fiery furnace. Paper. 112 pages.   MP-625

Leon Smith

Dennis Bashor

MARTHA BOLTON is no newcomer to the field of humor writing. Her credits include an award-winning newspaper column titled "The Cost of Living"; has gag-written for cartoonist Bill Hoest; currently writes for Bob Hope and other top comedians. Martha is a member of the National League of American Pen Women, Inc., International Women's Writing Guild, and the National Speakers Association.

In the religious field, Martha Bolton has been published in many periodicals and is herself a committed Christian and churchwoman. The situations and truths pictured in A FUNNY THING . . . could only have been written by one who knows her Bible and the human foibles of the Christian life.

ISBN 083-419-0842

9 780834 190849